Summary

of

Seth Godin's

Linchpin

Are You Indispensable?

by
Swift Reads

Table of Contents

Overview

Linchpin: Are You Indispensable? (2010) shows entrepreneurs and everyday workers alike how to become vital members of their professional fields. Author Seth Godin argues that the business world no longer profits by filling its rosters with cookie-cutter employees who meet minimum production levels. Instead, companies need forward-thinking employees who are able to spot problems and create solutions even when they aren't explicitly asked to do extra work. Linchpins, or workers who are able to use creativity and ingenuity to help their employers, not only gain the respect of their superiors and colleagues, but also become key parts of their company's continued success. By giving additional value to their employers without asking for commensurate compensation, linchpins make any field of work into an art. Becoming a company linchpin doesn't guarantee that a worker is irreplaceable, but it does guarantee professional security in the form of new job offers and increased reputation.

Since the nineteenth century, workers in both factory and office settings have been trained to follow orders, get good performance reviews, and fulfill quotas. Manufacturing jobs are no longer the only positions that use factory standards to ensure efficiency. Call centers, fast food restaurants, and hospitals all train employees and future staff to be obedient in exchange for financial security.

Many have come to associate these obedient and passive behaviors with safety, since factory work for a long time provided families with money, food, access to healthcare, and promise of a decent pension. In the 2000s and 2010s, however, technological innovations and stagnant wages have shown that workers can no longer settle for complacency and mediocre performance. Average work makes any employee vulnerable to layoffs and dead-end jobs, because businesses can easily train a replacement. To achieve a better financial future and gain more work satisfaction, employees must learn how to tap into their imagination and ability to innovate.

Employees who choose to become linchpins need to determine what their talents are, and then use those abilities to better their companies in ways that others have not predicted or thought possible. Every worker has a natural talent; in most cases, that ability can be used to improve business practices. A barista at a coffee shop, for example, could use a proclivity for empathy and attentiveness to improve customers' experience. A local farmer could demonstrate a talent for agriculture by providing vegetables that taste better than the ones sold at the chain grocery store.

Linchpins must demonstrate proficiency in emotional labor — meaning that they have the ability to use empathy to connect with customers, coworkers, and bosses. Since customers want a personalized experience, simply responding to a complaint with a formulaic answer is not enough to ensure the consumer's satisfaction and continued loyalty. Workers must learn how to connect emotionally with customers and display passion among coworkers. Unenthusiastic workers quickly become average workers, failing to stand out to superiors.

The educational system and the business world still encourage people to conform and follow orders. Linchpins, however, resist the urge to settle for mediocrity. By bringing humanity, creativity, charity, and passion to work, anyone can learn to become a worker who's central to their company's success.

Key Insights

1. Companies risk vulnerability to competitors when they rely on an easily trained labor force.

2. The internet has forced professionals to specialize and show individuality to remain competitive.

3. Linchpins forge maps that others can follow, rather than waiting for explicit instructions.

4. Productive employees silence their inner critics so that they can create good work.

5. Ambitious employees don't obtain their ideal careers by using conventional job-hunting methods.

6. Successful creators are driven not by money, but by the desire to see more art in the world.

7. Daily work chores can pile up, preventing linchpins from completing more important tasks.

8. Experts must use their knowledge insightfully and mentor inexperienced workers if they hope to be useful to employers.

Key Insight 1

Companies risk vulnerability to competitors when they rely on an easily trained labor force.

Analysis

If the tasks employees are required to perform can be taught easily to everyday hires, then a competitor could quickly figure out how to launch a similar business and profit off the same market. Hiring intuitive, motivated employees may make it harder to pay low wages, but those workers will help the company come up with original strategies for attracting clients and outperforming competitors. Businesses should strive to hire linchpins for most, if not all, positions if they want to stand out from other companies.

When looking for linchpins, companies should seek out employees who possess the skill set that will best benefit the business. Knowing what skill set to look for is especially important when hiring managers. In *Blitzscaling: The Lightning-Fast Path To Building Massively Valuable Companies* (2018), authors Reid Hoffman and Chris Yeh explain that massively successful corporations look for managers with a record of helping similar companies. Some professionals specialize in helping smaller companies, like those with fewer than 20 employees, and some do best when helping corporations with well over a thousand employees. If companies hire managers whose expertise lies in a different development stage or industry, the professionals likely will do their best, but won't be able to fully use their skills to their company's advantage.

A company may have to consider letting go of certain linchpins if the business shifts industries or continues expanding. An executive who was once effective may only be able to help grow a company to a certain extent, and will need to step aside if the business wants to capture further market share. Good managers will know what domains they are most skilled in, and will understand when the company has outgrown the help they can provide.

Key Insight 2

The internet has forced professionals to specialize and show individuality to remain competitive.

Analysis

The internet's accessibility has made it easier for some creatives to make a living; it has also increased the number of innovators vying for online fame and fortune. A piano player who wants to gain followers on YouTube will not only have to demonstrate great skill, but will have to put on a better show than other talented pianists competing for an audience on YouTube. Mediocre performers should either work to improve their skills, or consider whether they have another talent they could use to set themselves apart.

Innovative people can easily kill their motivation and confidence if they constantly strive to beat everyone in their field, because there will always be someone better. Instead of making a comparison to the standards of the masters in their profession, they should work on improving their own performance on a daily basis. In *The Slight Edge: Turning Simple Disciplines Into Massive Success & Happiness* (2005), author Jeff Olson explains that practicing a skill daily can eventually yield massive results. Skills will snowball as the potential linchpin moves past the basics and gains mastery. Olson argues that many people aren't willing to commit to a daily practice, and so give up the potential rewards they could reap by simply working on a skill every day. Those who do commit to improving themselves daily, then, will quickly outstrip their coworkers and attract the attention of their superiors. For example, if an aspiring linchpin knows that she is not the top professional in her field, she can start small by trying to outperform herself each day. Slowly, she will be able to outpace the other workers in her region, before eventually making a name for herself on a national level.

Key Insight 3

Linchpins forge maps that others can follow, rather than waiting for explicit instructions.

Analysis

Former Google executive Marissa Mayer wasn't explicitly hired to improve the website's user interface. Despite that, she used her artistic insights to note that Google's main search page would be more attractive if it were minimalist. She even tallied the number of words on the main search page so that the interface would look cleaner. Since she took action without needing explicit instruction, Mayer made herself more valuable to her employer than a colleague who simply performed well at assigned tasks.

Aspiring linchpins stuck in an entry-level position should look for chances to step up and take on leadership roles, even if it's only when the boss is out of the office. Asking for more responsibility can especially benefit groups of underrepresented workers, like women, who may not be given as many leadership opportunities. In a 2015 *Guardian* article, reporter Lottie O'Conor encourages women to volunteer to lead their teams when the boss goes on vacation. Acting as a substitute manager shows that an employee is ready for a supervisor position, and provides the opportunity to interact with executives. A temporary leadership position additionally allows an employee to make beneficial changes that the boss may not have considered. If employees are given the chance to take on a temporary leadership role, they should remember to act decisively, instead of second-guessing their decisions. Constantly seeking feedback, especially from the absent boss, may lead superiors to believe an employee is unprepared to take on future responsibilities. By being assertive and volunteering to lead, employees can set themselves apart and demonstrate that they want to give more to the company than the bare minimum.

Key Insight 4

Productive employees silence their inner critics so that they can create good work.

Analysis

Most people have an inner voice that tells them they shouldn't try new, innovative strategies. That voice also says they'll fail if they attempt to take on new roles in their profession. That inner critic, however, is coming from the "lizard brain," or the fearful parts of the mind content to sacrifice the possibility of success for the promise of safety. Aspiring linchpins should learn to accept that rejection is part of the creative process, and give themselves permission to fail as long as they commit to trying their hardest.

In some cases, the critical inner voice can be fueled by the negativity absorbed from colleagues and family members. In *The Energy Bus: 10 Rules to Fuel Your Life, Work, and Team with Positive Energy* (2007), author Jon Gordon weaves an allegorical tale in which an unhappy and failing supervisor uses positivity to turn his life around. When the main character, George, attempts to rally his department on a stalled project, he meets resistance from the negative members of his team.

Those employees demonstrate that they are rooting for George's failure, causing him to absorb their rotten attitudes and doubt his own abilities. Through George, Gordon makes the point that employees who are consistently surrounded by naysayers have a harder time maintaining motivation and confidence, and may become negative themselves. Bad attitudes are contagious, and should be stamped out whenever possible. For example, if an employee realizes that a coworker's negativity is affecting her work, she should confront the colleague about the behavior and attempt to change it. If the behavior can't be changed, she should limit the time she spends around that employee; management may additionally have to consider whether the negative worker has to be let go for the sake of others in the office.

Key Insight 5

Ambitious employees don't obtain their ideal careers by using conventional job-hunting methods.

Analysis

When professionals look for a new job, they often turn to one of the most familiar job-hunting tools: resumes. Resumes aren't the most effective way for a prospective hire to showcase personality or skills. Since so many job-hunters use resumes, the documents can start to blur together for hiring managers, making it easy for a talented applicant to be overlooked. Resumes additionally give employers the impression that a candidate is only skilled in the listed abilities, which may negate the chances of landing the job. Professionals should focus on cultivating their online reputation when looking for jobs, rather than handing out resumes to businesses.

Resumes aren't the only conventional job-hunting method to avoid. Linchpins should additionally beware the temptation to wait for an open position before attempting to land a job at their dream company. In *What Color Is Your Parachute? 2019: A Practical Manual for Job-Hunters and*

Career-Changers (2018), job seekers are advised to create a list of companies they might be interested in, instead of sifting through job postings for the perfect opportunity. Once job-hunters have a list of attractive businesses where they could be happy, they can learn more about those organizations, whittle down the list to a few potential employers, and forge connections with people who already work for those companies. An ambitious job-hunter can then use relationships with those employees to meet members of the hiring committee, offer help on a volunteer basis, or even convince an executive to create a custom position that utilizes the job-hunter's skills. Professionals who seek out specific companies set themselves apart as discerning and dedicated. Even if a company is unable to hire a candidate, executives may be so impressed that they consider the professional for future opportunities, or recommend a job at a related organization. As long as applicants are mindful of others' time and don't display a superficial knowledge of the company, they are likely to leave a positive impression that can help in future job hunts.

Key Insight 6

Successful creators are driven not by money, but by the desire to see more art in the world.

Analysis

When Shepard Fairey created an artistic representation of former President Barack Obama during his 2008 campaign, he didn't intend to sell artwork for money. Yet after the image became popular, he was able to find new clients and fans who were interested in his style. Talented people can easily replicate original designs to make a modest income if money is their only goal. Creators who complete projects because they love their work, however, are capable of groundbreaking innovations that capture the attention of the marketplace. Linchpins can still care about obtaining a decent salary, but completing projects with the sole intention of making money will kill creativity and result in bland final products.

If a creator distributes a more elaborate work of art for free, for example, he may find that the work quickly attracts more attention and praise than he anticipated. As the product accumulates fans, it may inspire spin-off projects and responsibilities that take up more of his time. In those cases, creators may need to adjust deadlines for future products to ensure they still meet the same quality standards. In 2017, Dan Salvato, a programmer and video game designer, released a free visual horror novel called *Doki Doki Literature Club (DDLC)*. The game quickly garnered a dedicated fan base because of its well-written plot and innovative gaming components. Salvato, who dropped a hint in the game that he would be releasing another title in 2018, recently let fans know that he didn't expect *DDLC* to become so popular. Much of his attention in 2018 was diverted toward providing additional content for *DDLC* fans, such as posters and other merchandise based on the game's artwork. He told followers that he still expected to release future games, but that his schedule had been pushed back to ensure that his next projects were completed with the same care as *DDLC*. Salvato could have leveraged the success of *DDLC* to release a substandard product for quick profit, but that would likely have tarnished his reputation, making it harder for him to grow his audience. By adjusting his deadlines, Salvato showed his followers that he is committed to delivering quality art on a consistent basis.

Key Insight 7

Daily work chores can pile up, preventing linchpins from completing more important tasks.

Analysis

If professionals are constantly busy putting out the small fires that arise during the day, they won't have time to focus on bigger projects that require patience and concentration. Mundane chores can sap creativity and take up time, making it easier for employees to sink into complacency and only meet standard productivity requirements. If possible, an aspiring linchpin should minimize the time those responsibilities take up, perhaps by delegating smaller tasks to other team members.

Ambitious employees can additionally free up time for large projects by avoiding bad work habits that lead to unintentional delays. A *New York Times* guide on workplace productivity points out that many employees mistakenly believe multitasking can help a worker get more done throughout the day. Instead, multitasking leads to broken concentration and lengthens the amount of time it takes to complete a project. Earl K. Miller, a Massachusetts Institute of Technology neuroscience professor, told the *Times* that human minds simply don't have the ability to seamlessly perform two streams of thought at one time; no one, he said, is capable of true multitasking. Workers should focus on one task at a time, and give themselves the space to dedicate their attention fully to it. Once they've completed a goal, or reached a stopping point, they can move on to another task on their to-do list.

Key Insight 8

Experts must use their knowledge insightfully and mentor inexperienced workers if they hope to be useful to employers.

Analysis

Being an expert on a specific subject is no longer enough to ensure a continued position at a company. Thanks to the internet, anyone can obtain answers to questions that require specialized knowledge. If experts want to remain relevant in their fields, they need to do more than regurgitate facts. They must be able to use their knowledge to create strategies that improve the company. Experts should offer their accumulated wisdom to younger professionals who are still trying to learn tools of the trade.

Ambitious experts who offer mentorship along with knowledge often get tapped for leadership positions within companies. When that happens, those experts will eventually deal with problems that lie outside of their specialization, and will have to consider turning to more experienced professionals for advice. In a 2015 *Harvard Business Review* article, Wanda T. Wallace and David Creelman argue that many promising leaders become despondent or even angry when they realize they are no longer the top expert in their department. They may be tempted to achieve mastery in all the fields that their position oversees to compensate for their lack of knowledge. It's simply not feasible, however, for someone to obtain specialization in a few days or months. The depth of a person's knowledge was not what made that person a leader; instead, it was the ability to leverage knowledge. Experts should be willing to hire people who have more knowledge and experience than they do. Doing so allows a leader to bypass the time-consuming task of gaining new specializations.

Important People

Seth Godin is an entrepreneur and author who has written more than a dozen books including *The Dip: A Little Book That Teaches You When to Quit* (2007) and *Purple Cow: Transform Your Business by Being Remarkable* (2003).

Marissa Mayer is an executive who specializes in helping technology companies. She previously served as a Google executive, as well president of Yahoo!

Shepard Fairey is an illustrator and graphic designer who became well known after creating an artistic depiction of Barack Obama during his first presidential campaign.

Author's Style

Linchpin is written in a manifesto style, filled with proclamations about the traits that notable employees cultivate to set themselves apart from their coworkers. Throughout, Godin uses stories from the professional relationships he's developed in his own life to illustrate how following the status quo can ultimately hurt an employee's future chances. Sometimes, Godin's enthusiastic belief in the ability of his readers to succeed leads him to make questionable assertions. For example, in one chapter, he claims without providing evidence that the placebo effect can cure cancer.

Linchpin contains 12 chapters, an introduction and summary. The chapters are broken into numerous subsections, most of which contain only a few sentences. Some chapters contain simplistic drawings and diagrams. At the end of the book, Godin provides a list of books he references throughout his work that may be useful to readers aiming to become insightful, essential employees.

Author's Perspective

Although standing out as a professional is a skill that any worker can learn, Godin points out that very few employees ever find the courage to become truly indispensable. Despite their inherent potential, most employees seem content simply to follow instructions and collect a paycheck. The widespread tendency among workers to accept mediocrity leaves ample opportunity for ambitious professionals to fill gaps that haven't been explicitly identified by company owners and managers. By looking for opportunities to solve problems and improve productivity without being asked, employees can create a reputation for competency.

Godin argues that most professionals choose to be average because they have been taught from an early age that thwarting social or business convention is a path to financial ruin. To illustrate why most workers are prone to conformity, Godin turns to economic philosophers like Karl Marx and Adam Smith, contrasting their wisdom with modern business practices.

Although he criticizes capitalism and common factory practices throughout *Linchpin*, Godin does not advocate for any larger change in the financial system. Nor does he believe that unhappy employees should immediately find new jobs upon reading his book. Rather, he believes that professionals should take advantage of the gaps created by outdated business mores. By evaluating where and how they can make a difference, learning how to take measured risks, and avoiding the urge to stay average, professionals can slowly gain notice at their companies and achieve financial security.

Printed in Great Britain
by Amazon